S0-ANO-357

BRININSTOOL + LYNCH: BUILDING ON MODERNISM

First published in the United States of America by Edizioni Press, Inc.
469 West 21st Street New York, New York 10011, www.edizionipress.com

ISBN: 1-931536-06-6
Library of Congress Catalogue Card Number: 2001099233

Printed in Italy

Design: William van Roden
Editor: Jamie Schwartz
Editorial Assistants: Sarah Palmer, Aaron Seward

BUILDING ON MODERNISM

by Raul A. Barreneche

There's good news and bad news about modernism's ongoing resurgence. The good news is that after decades of enduring a bad rap at the hands of postmodernism, the lost language of Mies van der Rohe and Le Corbusier is back. Designers like Vernor Panton, Harry Bertoia, Florence Knoll, and the Eames are now household names, thanks to the embrace of the fashion world and a newfound interest in domesticity. The bad news is that this rediscovery of modernism is mostly a matter of style, not substance. Youngsters enamored by the sleek lines of a bent plywood chair have no idea that it was the product of a design revolution in the early 20th century, born of an interest in the mass production and distribution of design, social equity, and global equality. The early modernists were not interested in making expensive furniture on which to lounge in designer outfits.

In America these days, the design of affordable modern furniture and objects has largely been left to big retailers like IKEA and Target; architecturally, there are few firms who consistently design conscientious but high-style projects. For architects in other parts of the world—in Sweden, for instance—such a combination is second nature; but most American clients think they have to sacrifice good design to meet the bottom line, and they often feel more at home with the comfort of historically minded architecture. Sadly, serious modern architecture in this country has become the province of the well-to-do.

The work of Brininstool + Lynch, an energetic firm in Chicago, is in many ways an exception to this status quo. Working in a city that was once the cradle of American architecture—the birthplace of the skyscraper and other architectural firsts—but lately a wasteland of interesting new design, David Brininstool and Brad Lynch have successfully cast off modernism's sheen of pretension and fashionableness. They've returned instead to its origins as investigative, provocative, and affordable architecture.

Like the early modernists, Brininstool + Lynch buildstet exceptional buildings from ordinary, even humble elements. Their palette is limited, with materials that recur throughout projects of different scales and types: concrete block, blond maple, plastic laminates, translucent fiberglass, and plywood. "Materials—an integral part of the design process—are selected for compatibility and affordability, never in imitation of other materials," Brad Lynch explains. The risk of using these materials isn't that they would be taken as substitutes for more expensive elements, but rather that they would be fetishized and made trendy. So many projects designed by architects in Southern California—thanks to Frank Gehry, who, in his early years, elevated plywood, raw concrete block, and chain-link fencing to high art—have repeated this palette endlessly. As a result, the office of almost every self-consciously cool film production office, art gallery, and loft in Santa Monica or Venice looks the same, and I, for one, can't bear the sight of another.

Brininstool + Lynch's work is markedly different from that of their West Coast counterparts. Though they use the same modest materials, they make much more elegant, dignified spaces because they treat these elements with respect, as if they were costlier marble or mahogany. Their work is not about making jarring, cacophonous collages of low-cost industrial parts; it's about creating sophisticated spaces while letting the richness of materials come through—the unmistakable grain of a sheet of plywood or the porous texture of a concrete block surface. Though the parts may be gritty, the whole is always sleek and self-assured—and made with an eye towards affordability. As David Brininstool explains, "We do not create designs that cannot be effectively constructed, nor do we spend our way out of design problems." Materials are important, but they are not the primary focus of their work; space and light are more important considerations.

Like many architects, Brininstool + Lynch first made their mark designing houses. But the success of their early domestic projects, often modestly scaled homes in the emerging urban neighborhoods of Chicago, led to more high-end residential commissions—weekend houses and condos in lakefront high-rises—and eventually to larger commercial and institutional work. Even in their bigger-budget projects, they display the same commitment to crafting clean, sophisticated spaces and exploring affordable materials. In their renovation of the Racine Art Museum, cheap, durable acrylic panels wrap an existing limestone building to create a luminous new skin. In a new residential tower on Michigan Avenue in Chicago, aluminum, glass, and a scrim of woven wire comprise the building's public face.

In some of their work, however, new materials take a back seat to the existing architecture, as in the Perimeter Gallery, housed in an historic loft space in Chicago's River North neighborhood. Faced with a constricting budget, Brininstool + Lynch chose to let the elements of the existing loft—exposed wooden ceiling joists and brick walls—define the character of their renovation. Rather than fussing with new materials, the architects defined spaces within the existing shell with planes of ordinary drywall. Clever details, including suspended wall panels on wooden pedestals, which create the illusion that they float above the floor, and slots inserted between wall panels to bring daylight further into the gallery, make the ordinary a touch more extraordinary.

It's a testament to the simple grace of Brininstool + Lynch's work that other visual practitioners, including gallery owners and graphic designers, are their clients. But of course, it's not just similarly minded designers and artists who find their work compelling. Institutions, homeowners, even commercial and residential developers—the toughest clients to sell on the power of design—are all sold on the architects' skillful solutions and simple aesthetics.

In an age when clients either care nothing about design or care only about its most superficial elements, Brininstool + Lynch's work provides a happy marriage of substance and style. There is nothing trendy about their design; they are not promoting an aesthetic or intellectual agenda, and are certainly not jumping on the ingratiating bandwagon of so-called "blob" design. With its attention to solving functional and financial problems with aesthetic aplomb, their architecture gets back to the sadly overlooked roots of the modern movement. They are the successors of the early modernists and the standard bearers of affordable, accessible modernism at the beginning of the 21st century.

"Architecture should be a safe haven for one's intellect, and a comfort to one's soul," says Brad Lynch. "It should inspire." And their work certainly does. ■

Location	Chicago, Illinois
Design	1993
Construction	1993-1994
Materials	Concrete foundation, concrete block, steel, cedar siding, wood framing, birch and maple panels and millwork, maple flooring, Vermont slate
Area	3,000 square feet

THOMPSON RESIDENCE

THOMPSON RESIDENCE

Brininstool + Lynch designed a freestanding three-story house to fit into the neither gentrified nor drab surroundings of Chicago's Bucktown neighborhood.

Since the entrance to the house is recessed four feet below the sidewalk, the entry foyer is located at the basement level, along with a guest room and family room facing a rear yard, and a study facing a side yard. A maple staircase wrapped in thin walls of birch plywood leads to the living room, dining room, and kitchen on the second floor. A small balcony off the living room offers views of the landscaped backyard. Separating the living room and kitchen is a two-story light well, topped by a barrel vaulted skylight and a lay-light of translucent glass on the interior that can be artificially lit.

On the third floor, a hallway bridges the divide created by the light well extending up to the roof. The front end of the house contains the master bedroom; the walk-in closet and master bath are accessed from a small hallway to the north of the bedroom. A panel of translucent fiberglass in the wall over the bathtub allows the bathroom to borrow natural light from the light well. The child's bedroom and bath are at the rear of the top floor.

The interiors are finished in painted drywall, maple, birch plywood, slate, ceramic tile, and carpet. All of the exterior concrete block walls are exposed on the interior. Central core walls and dividers are constructed of wood studs and finished in drywall. In the living room and dining room, large, translucent fiberglass panels set into the exterior walls can be back-lit from outside to create a soft glow indoors. Facing Page: **Stairs leading to the living room at the rear of the house are visible from the front entrance at the lower level. Here, the architects used a variety of materials to explore ideas of compression, with the roof of the entry, and release, as the ceiling at the stair rises to meet the high ceilings of the open living room.**

Facing Page: **Fiberglass panels on the south wall of the living room, as well as a two-story light well allow sunlight to flood the space.** This Page: **The living room opens onto a balcony, overlooking the garden in back of the house. The family room is visible through the windows at basement level.**

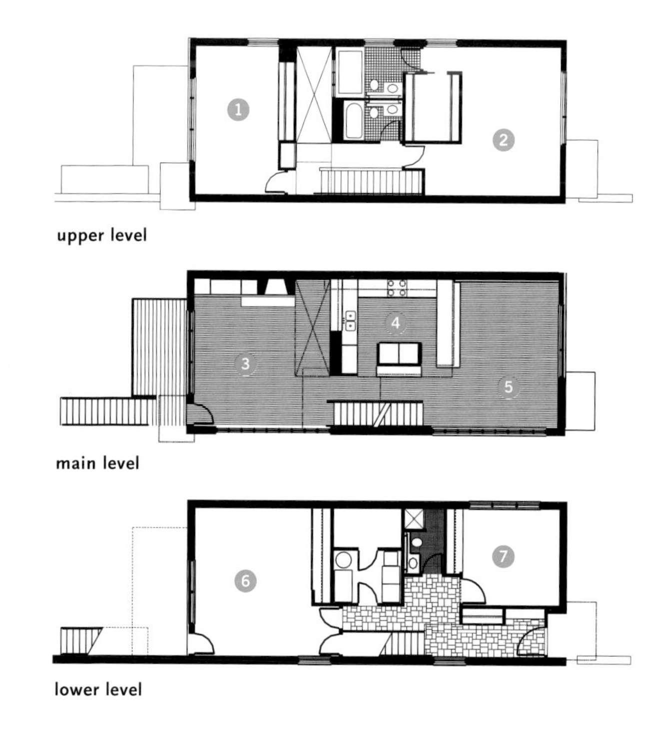

1. Bedroom
2. Master Bedroom
3. Living Room
4. Kitchen
5. Dining Room
6. Family Room
7. Study

Facing Page: **(Top) The open layout allows for easy circulation between the kitchen and living room. The designers used birch and maple plywood for the millwork and cabinets in the kitchen. (Bottom) The walls of the stairwell are finished in the same plywood used throughout the kitchen to create an integrated design.**

Location	Bridgman, Michigan
Design	1994
Construction	1994-1995
Materials	Concrete, slate, granite, wood framing, cedar shake and exterior siding, wood windows and doors, maple millwork and flooring, plaster veneer
Area	1,825 square feet

BURKHARDT RESIDENCE

BURKHARDT RESIDENCE

The architects designed this 1,825-square-foot weekend retreat, overlooking a wooded valley in the dunes on Lake Michigan's shore, to harmonize with the natural environment. Set at an intermediate level against a steeply sloped dune forest, the house is outfitted with a boardwalk leading up to the front door. The boardwalk's axis to the entry implies that it continues through the house to the porch on the other side. The entire structure acts as a viewing platform made of simple forms and natural materials that minimize the home's intrusion on the environment. As many existing trees as possible were preserved, and new landscaping was added to screen the house from view.

The main entrance is reached from a secluded gravel lane, leading to the boardwalk—which acts as a sidewalk for the entry, elevated two feet above grade to align with the front door—and creates a visual axis aligning with a granite fireplace, screened-in porch, and the woods beyond. The entryway and kitchen were configured as maple-clad volumes set on a plane of Vermont slate tiles.

The program called for a flexible, low-maintenance home—containing, among other spaces, two bedrooms, a study, and a sleeping loft—with maximum exposure to the outdoors. A 14-foot-high glass wall in the living room brings the surrounding woods inside, as do carefully placed windows in the master shower and bath. To further emphasize connections between indoors and outdoors, the designers used similar materials on the exterior and interior. For example, the cedar shake used on the exterior also sheaths interior volumes, and a wood-sided half wall extending along the boardwalk makes a further connection between the fabric of the house and the outdoors.

The architects custom designed sliding door panels of translucent acrylic set into wood frames and operable translucent shoji screens. Used throughout the house, the screens can create privacy or leave interior spaces open. The rest of the material palette—maple plywood and flooring, granite, and slate—accommodates these Asian-inspired elements, while also acknowledging the owner's native Vermont. Previous Pages: **The curved, up-lighted ceiling of the kitchen and living room ascends to a height of 18 feet.** Facing Page: **A window seat at the back of the living room, designed as part of the fireplace wall, provides space for wood storage. The exterior wall is finished in cedar shingles and juxtaposed with the sliding glass door.**

A boardwalk leads to the entrance, which is aligned with the fireplace and the back porch beyond. As visitors approach the house, they can see the maple volumes of the kitchen through the large windows.

Facing Page: **The raised slate entry is echoed at the living room fireplace, composed of a honed granite base and a slate hearth.** This Page: **(Top) This section cuts through the boardwalk, entry, living room, and porch. Note the ceiling configuration and the cove provided for indirect light. (Bottom) This floor plan shows the shower, north of the boardwalk, and the exterior stair leading to the basement.**

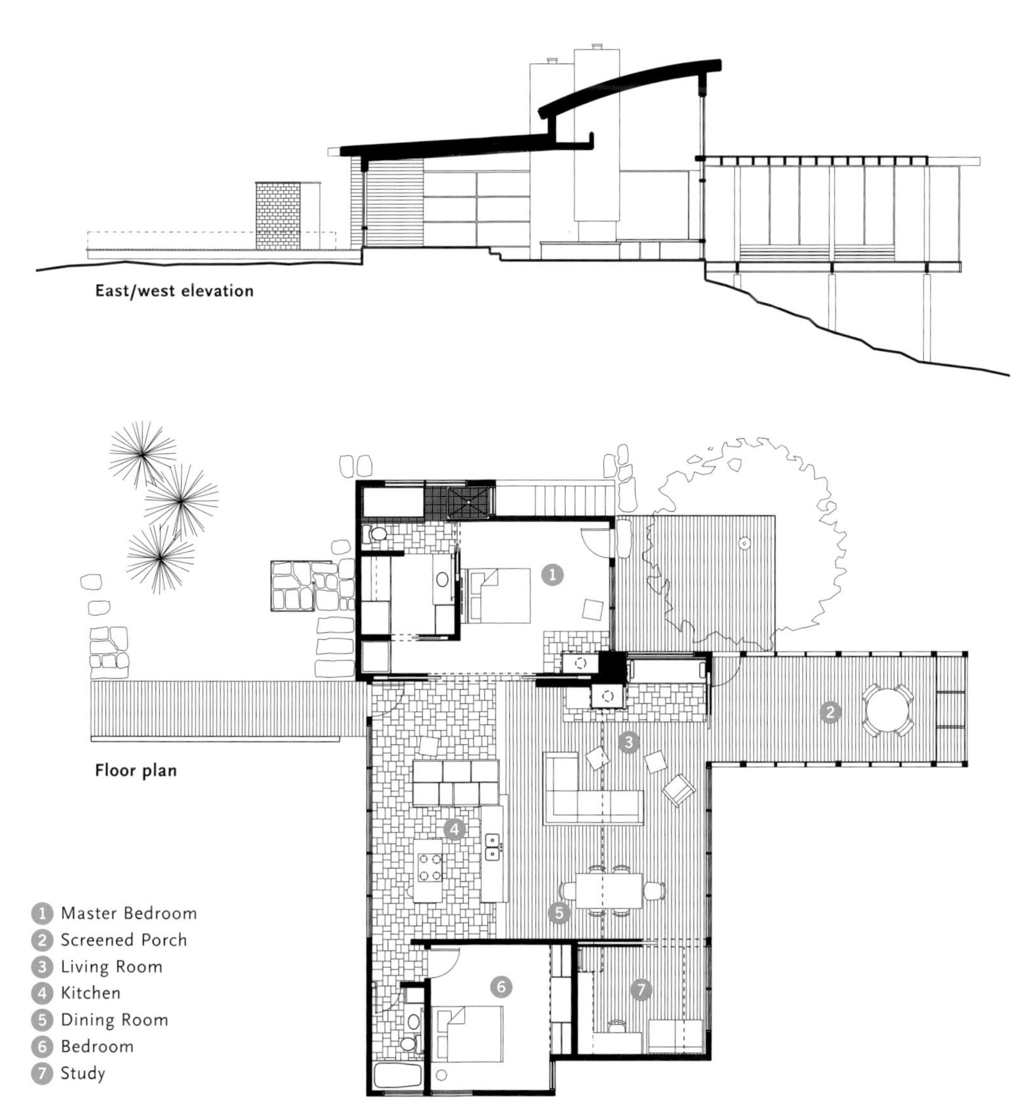

Location	Chicago, Illinois
Design	1996
Construction	1996
Materials	Gypsum board systems, steel and wood framing, birch panels and millwork, laminated translucent glass
Area	2,700 square feet

PERIMETER GALLERY CHICAGO

PERIMETER GALLERY: CHICAGO

Brininstoool + Lynch created an optimal environment for viewing art at the Perimeter Gallery in Chicago's River North neighborhood. The architects were challenged to accomplish the design and construction within a limited schedule and budget. To achieve both objectives, they made creative use of existing and new materials for the long, narrow loft space in an old printing building.

To keep costs down, the architects repaired the existing wood floors and exposed wood ceilings. A series of partitions, braced with maple plywood, is located along a floating plywood-mounted gypsum board wall, and serves to separate the space into smaller "galleries" within the gallery, creating intimate zones appropriate for viewing a variety of art. An angled wall, also made of gypsum board on plywood with metal studs, runs north-south through the space and is back-lit with incandescent tubes, to draw visitors into the gallery.

The director's office at the rear of the gallery features a translucent glass panel in the door, which faces the pubic spaces. The east wall of the office has a large punched opening with two panels of butt-glazed translucent glass. Since there were no windows to the outside from the director's office, the architects used the translucent glass to bring in borrowed natural and artificial light while maintaining privacy. The director brought his old furniture with him; the designers added basic plastic laminate shelving, shelf brackets, and black metal filing cabinets to the office.

The centrally located reception desk allows the receptionist to visually monitor activity throughout the gallery, including a staircase that leads to a smaller, 550-square-foot exhibit space and storage area. A ceiling soffit defines the entrance and creates a path from outside the front door into the center of the gallery. A lowered soffit area over the reception desk emphasizes that relationship, and separates the reception area from the gallery space. The assistant director's office is part of an alcove behind the reception desk, where office equipment, lateral files, and bookshelves are kept.

Facing Page: **From the street, pedestrians can view the exhibited artwork through the front window of the gallery.**

Perimeter Gallery

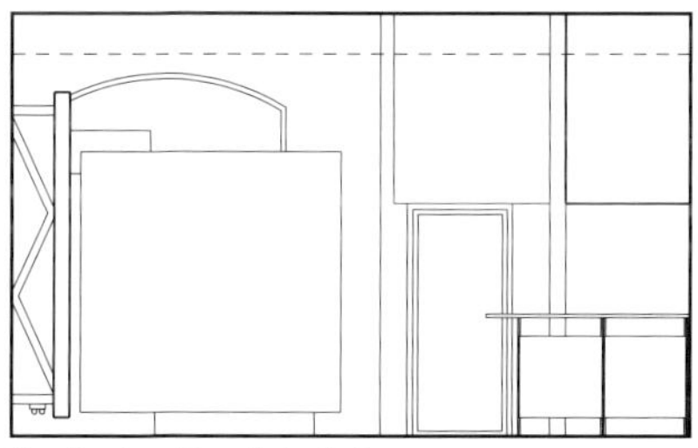

South elevation (interior)

1. Director's Office
2. Reception
3. Assistant Director's Office

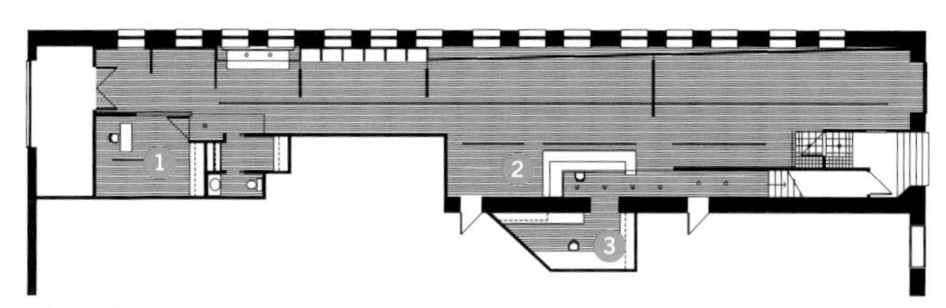

Floor plan

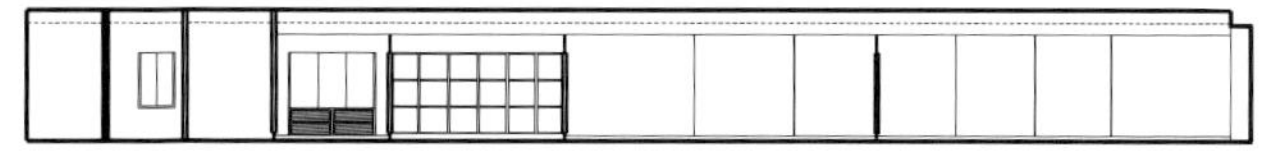

East elevation (interior)

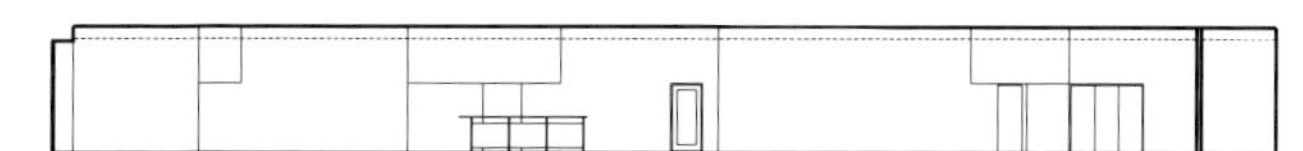

West elevation (interior)

Facing Page: **Three floating partition walls can be rearranged to accommodate changing exhibitions. Display shelving begins at the north end of the angled wall.** This Page: **(Top) The floating partition walls create a vignette of sub-spaces within the gallery, allowing for the presentation of varied artwork.**

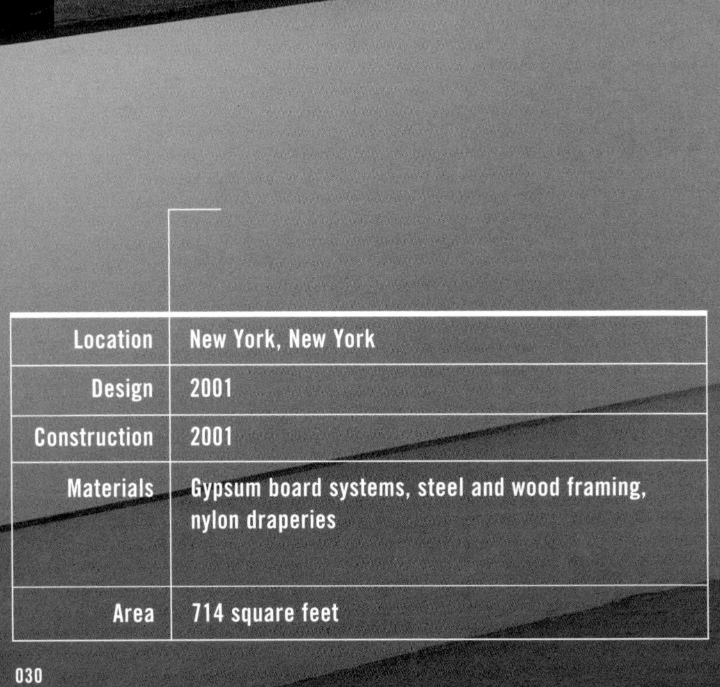

Location	New York, New York
Design	2001
Construction	2001
Materials	Gypsum board systems, steel and wood framing, nylon draperies
Area	714 square feet

PERIMETER GALLERY NEW YORK

PERIMETER GALLERY: NEW YORK

Brininstool + Lynch designed a satellite Perimeter Gallery in New York's Chelsea neighborhood, working within the tight constraints of a 714-square-foot space, a 30-day design and construction schedule, and a $15,000 budget. The gallery's director wanted to create a meditative, salon-like environment for viewing art.

Given the extremely limited budget, the architects focused on painting the space and installing new lighting and drapes to hide existing filing cabinets, flat files, kitchen cabinets, and storage areas. They defined a new environment within the gallery by floating a gypsum-board wall between the ceiling beams and the floor, tilting it at a slight angle against the length of the space and column. At the end of the gallery, an additional wall of the same height, placed perpendicular and a few degrees off, uses exaggerated perspective to create the illusion of a larger space. A small gap between the two walls lets indirect natural light in from the large windows without affecting the lighting of the artwork on the walls. Facing Page. **(Center) A built-out column and a partition wall divide storage space, on the right, from the gallery, on the left.**

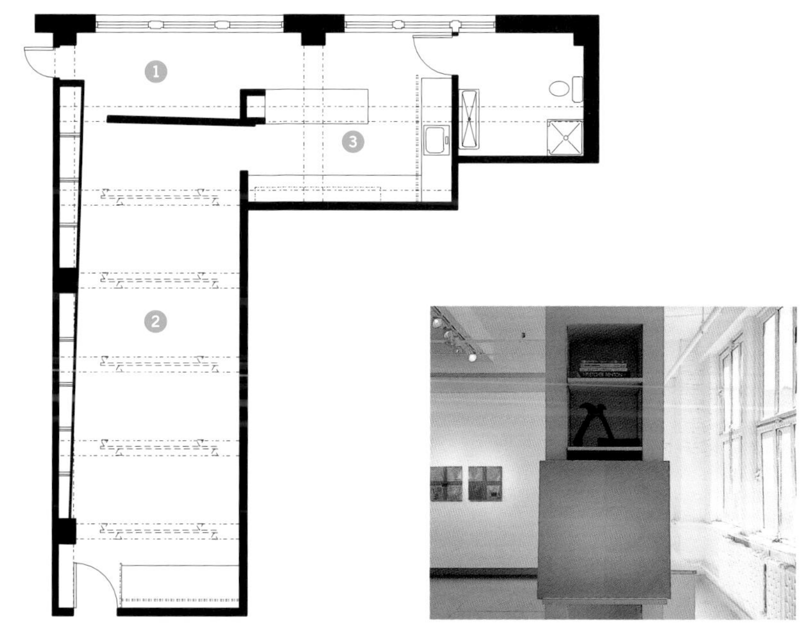

Floor plan

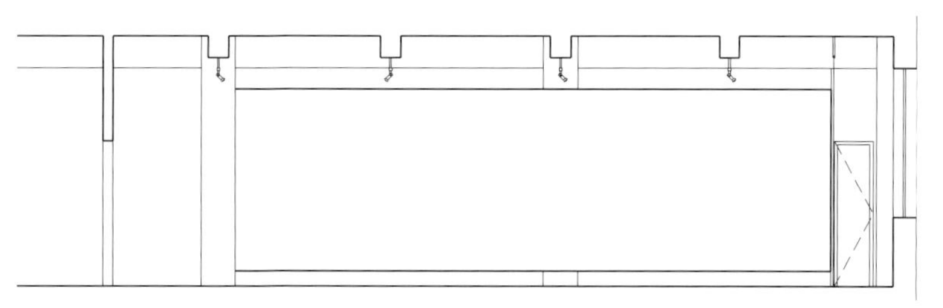

East elevation (interior)

Behind the partition wall is storage space, as well as windows that provide some natural light within the gallery. The entrance to the office and kitchen is located between the wall on the right and the partition wall.

Location	Chicago, Illinois
Design	1997
Construction	1997
Materials	Metal stud framing, sand-blasted translucent glass, fabric panels, maple panels and millwork
Area	1,250 square feet

CHICAGO RECORDING CO.

CHICAGO RECORDING CO.

The design for this post-production audio-to-film facility combines state-of-the-art technology with luxurious interiors and dramatic views of the city. The facility occupies 1,250 square feet on the third floor of a masonry loft building in Chicago's Streeterville neighborhood, and is shared by several divisions of the same company.

The program required a control room with a completely accurate, full-frequency audio monitoring environment to provide precise assessment of high-fidelity audio soundtracks. The location challenged the designers with its tight column grids and limited ceiling heights. To create the soundproof environment required by the client, the architects designed a space within the space: An interior structure, containing the control room and the studio, floats within the existing building, with isolation brackets attaching metal-stud framing to the building envelope.

The designers used sandblasted glass partitions to maintain an open atmosphere in the lobby and studio, which comprises the control room, recording studio, the client meeting area, and the equipment/machine room, while separating these areas from the entrance.

Music performances, voice performances, and voice-over work is done in the studio, which is acoustically isolated from the control room. The control room features a parabolic ceiling of maple plywood above the console area. This hovering ceiling plane conceals a video projector and indirect lighting fixtures, while directing sound to the rear of the room. Sound attenuation fabric, installed in panels over soundproof batting, conceals the speaker systems; carpeting and sheet rubber flooring control sound distribution in the space.

Film images, primarily for movies and commercials, can be projected onto the screen in the control room and given a soundtrack. Clients and engineers can also project images onto small monitors at desks scattered throughout the space. In addition, there is a private area where clients can meet, work, or make phone calls, as well as a small machine room where computer servers and racks of audio equipment are located.

All of the glazed openings in the facility are composed of at least two layers of 1/2-inch-thick glass, which are installed at canted angles in order to limit direct sound reflection from the glass. The architects installed the same glass on the interior surfaces of external windows. Throughout the studio are custom-designed elements, such as a glass, wood, and steel coffee table, built-in seating, and plastic laminate counter tops and workstations. The architects also incorporated custom millwork and cabinets made of maple, perforated metal, plastic laminate, and steel channel.

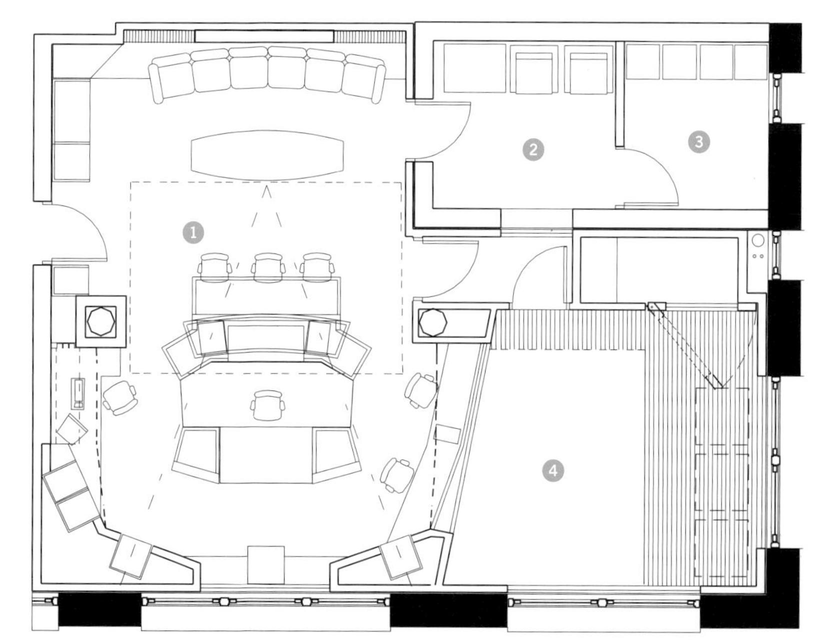

1 Control Room
2 Private Client Room
3 Equipment
4 Studio

A translucent glass wall separates the lobby from the studio, maintaining an open atmosphere in a facility that requires complex technical control.

CRC
CHICAGO RECORDING COMPANY
SONY

Facing Page: **The control room provides the main engineer's console and a viewing area for clients at the back wall.** This Page: **The large window shown here, behind the main engineer's console, can be blacked out with automatic shading systems. A projection screen is lowered over the glass partition wall while work is in progress.**

Location	Chicago, Illinois
Design	1996-1998
Construction	1997-1999 (addition, un-built)
Materials	RENOVATION Limestone, steel structure, aluminum replacement windows, stainless steel panels, granite, maple panels and millwork, translucent glass, veneer plaster ADDITION Steel structure, poured-in-place concrete, granite, stainless steel curtain wall, Cortan steel panels
Building area	RENOVATION 57,200 square feet, ADDITION 56,250 square feet

CORUS BANK HEADQUARTERS

CORUS BANK HEADQUARTERS

The new corporate headquarters of this large regional bank is located at a prominent six-corner intersection on the north side of Chicago. Brininstool + Lynch renovated the exterior of an existing five-story limestone structure and its 57,000-square-foot interior, and designed a new addition comprising another 56,000 square feet of space, which will include new corporate banking offices and computer facilities. A master plan designed by the firm will address the development of future building on the site.

The exterior of the existing 1920s building—originally built for a different bank—was clad in limestone that was improperly maintained over the years. The architects thoughtfully renovated the exterior to highlight its historic features, replacing the deteriorated limestone with new masonry and pointing, cleaning, and reconnecting salvageable limestone to the façade with new metal fasteners. They also replaced the structural steel behind the limestone façade, where it had deteriorated, and replaced damaged windows. All of the work adhered to the Secretary of the Interior's guidelines for historic structures.

The architects renovated the first and second floors to maintain the historic features of the original building's two-story Neo-Gothic banking lobby, which is crowned by a large skylight and overlooked by a mezzanine level that houses offices. They completely gutted the top three floors of the original building, which are V-shaped in plan—built around the large lobby skylight that caps the diamond-shaped second story roof—and reconfigured them into new executive offices. At the apex of the V are the conference rooms, bookshelves and storage, and service kitchens; the 30-foot-wide "wings" of the V feature a mix of open workstations, private offices, and conference rooms placed on either side of central corridors.

The private offices and conference rooms in the "wings" are enclosed with transparent glass panels that visually connect the interior spaces. Soffits above the central corridors, lower than the original ceiling height of nine feet, ten inches, at the exterior walls, contain removable glass panels that access lighting and mechanical equipment. The ends of workstations and desks maintain a height of 30 inches or lower so as not to exceed the height of the existing windowsills

The new design has its own language and identity, but respects the original architecture of its historic neighbor. The front façade features a custom-designed stainless steel storefront and curtain wall. Inside, the lobby floors and detailing around the elevators and doors are constructed of granite and stainless steel, while wall finishes are distressed steel. The architects custom designed all the millwork and cabinets from a more contemporary palette of maple, perforated metal, plastic laminate, aluminum channel, and slate.

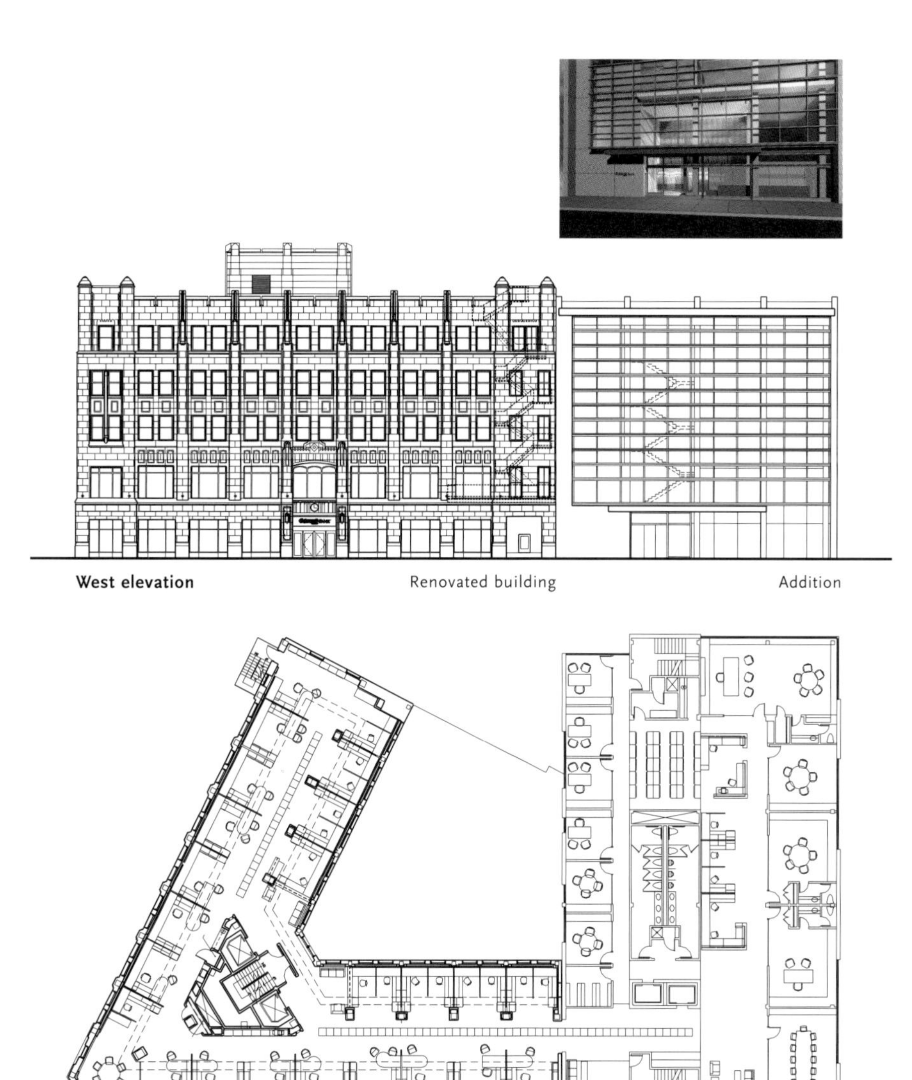

This Page: **(Top) This rendering shows the front façade of the new addition.**

Open work stations fill the west wall of the renovated building. Lowered ceiling areas contain HVAC and ambient light soffits are arranged around the perimeter.

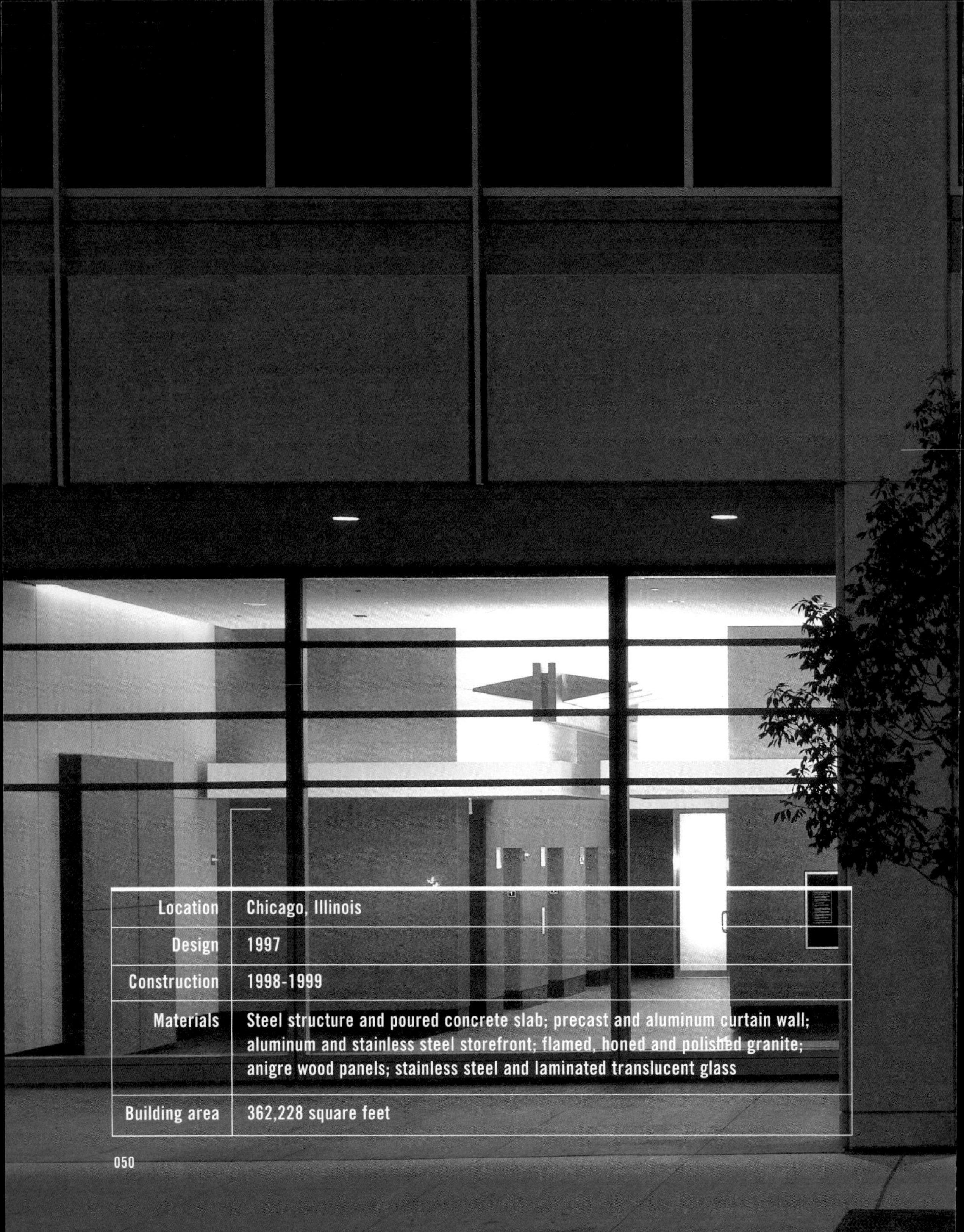

Location	Chicago, Illinois
Design	1997
Construction	1998-1999
Materials	Steel structure and poured concrete slab; precast and aluminum curtain wall; aluminum and stainless steel storefront; flamed, honed and polished granite; anigre wood panels; stainless steel and laminated translucent glass
Building area	362,228 square feet

UNION TOWER

UNION TOWER

Brininstool + Lynch was responsible for the conceptual design of Union Tower, a 330,000-square-foot office building sited on a corner lot in Chicago's West Loop area, as well as the design of its lobby. This project presented the challenge of creating an aesthetically pleasing design within existing zoning requirements, budget constraints, and a quick time frame.

The architects sought to emphasize the corner of the building by locating the lobby entrance at its apex. From there it was important to direct visitors to the elevator core. This was accomplished in two ways: first by articulating a pathway of granite slabs on the floor, and second by extending a translucent glass and steel lay-light fixture from the elevator core. The light fixture and soffits were designed to fit around diagonal, structural bracing at the base of the building. Facing page: The designers used flamed, honed, and polished granite on the walls and floors of the lobby. An etched pattern decorated the stainless steel elevator doors.

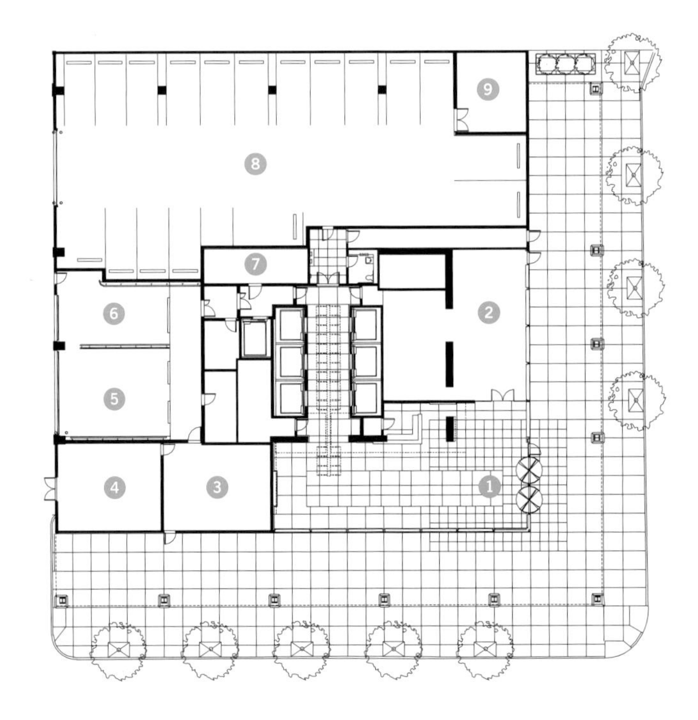

1. Lobby
2. Commercial
3. Vault
4. Switchgear Room
5. Truck Berths
6. Compactor
7. Phone/Data
8. Parking
9. Pump Room

The entrance to the elevator lobby is indicated by the glass and steel lay-light. Anigre wood, stainless steel, and granite are used on the reception desk and throughout the lobby.

Location	Chicago, Illinois
Design	1998
Construction	1999
Materials	Metal stud framing, gypsum board systems, sand-blasted translucent glass, custom maple millwork, perforated metal, plastic laminate, aluminum channel, slate, carpet, and vinyl floor covering
Area	5,500 square feet

LISKA & ASSOCIATES

LISKA & ASSOCIATES

Brininstool + Lynch created a calm and serene environment that promotes good corporate communication within this multimedia design firm. A set of transparent glass doors and side panels leads visitors from the elevator lobby into the reception area, which features a custom-designed desk of steel, maple panels, perforated metal, and slate.

Walls of sandblasted, translucent glass panels divide the reception area, conference rooms, and private offices from the large studio area where graphic designers work in freestanding, custom-designed workstations. These workstations preserve the open studio environment and maintain views of the city.

For the design studio, the architects designed modules, each composed of two workstations and two flat files, which sit in the middle of the floor without touching a wall. Each bay features a pair of anodized aluminum poles that bring power and communications cabling to the workstations from the ceiling. The black plastic laminate work surfaces are designed to hold large graphic layouts and computer monitors. Each workstation has a rectangular maple and aluminum cabinet for bookshelves, outlets for power and cabling, and recessed task lighting. Panels of perforated steel—which appear to float away from the glass partitions due to the use of rubber gaskets—function as lay-up surfaces for projects.

A large conference room, where client meetings and presentations and staff meetings are held, features a custom-designed aluminum conference table with pop-up power and communications portals for plugging in laptops and monitors. The designers used perforated metal panels mounted on the translucent glass wall as magnetic display surfaces for drawings. Another wall of floor-to-ceiling, porcelain-coated metal panels can be used as a magnetic display wall or as a marker board. A smaller conference room, fitted with the same metal panels, accommodates small in-house conferences and doubles as the office library. To the east of the kitchen is an area for light tables, the copier and fax machine, paper storage, and storage for books and manuals.

The interior palette is simple: white paint, maple, aluminum, glass, and off-gray carpet. The materials and colors are meant to enhance the open space. Facing Page: **(Top) Work stations in the studio area offer ample shelf space. The aluminum tube houses power and communications cables.**

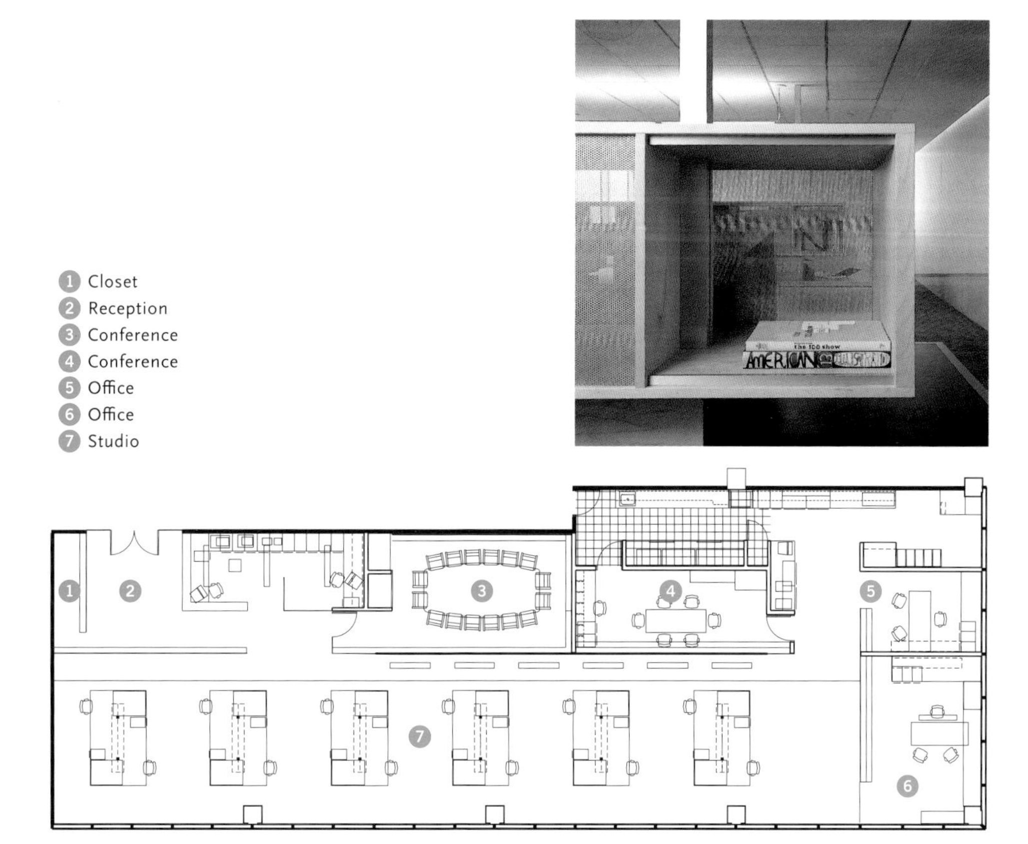

1 Closet
2 Reception
3 Conference
4 Conference
5 Office
6 Office
7 Studio

This Page: **The translucent glass wall in the foreground separates the reception area from the studio.**
Facing Page: **The glass wall at left separates the studio from the conference rooms. Employees use magnets to display work in progress on the metal panels affixed to the glass.**

This Page: **The reception desk is made of aluminum, maple, and slate. A cloak area is located to the right of the benches, behind the glass wall.** Facing Page: **The architects' plan preserved views and natural light for workstations in the studio.**

Location	McCordsville, Indiana
Design	1997-1998
Construction	1998-2000
Materials	Concrete, brick masonry, limestone, slate, granite, steel and wood framing, redwood and cedar siding, maple millwork and flooring, laminated translucent glass, plaster veneer, aluminum leaf
Building area	5,350 square feet

YAMAMOTO RESIDENCE

YAMAMOTO RESIDENCE

Brininstool + Lynch designed this 5,350-square-foot house, located on a cul-de-sac in suburban Indianapolis, as a serene environment for the display of art and a comfortable place for entertaining. The entry sequence is defined by a series of horizontal elements, including the garage, a brick garden wall, and an entrance canopy, which privatize and delineate the approach to the house. By setting the house as far away from the street as possible, the architects insulated it from the neighborhood's neo-traditional houses, while reducing the impact of their own design on that context. The intent is a calm juxtaposition of styles rather than a radical statement.

The house slowly opens to an influx of views and natural light. As one enters the foyer and looks down a long hallway, the woods are visible through windows in the living room. To the right of the entry is a smaller hallway that leads to a set of windows facing the side yard. The main rooms of the house all have views over a landscaped garden area and through the woods toward a lake.

A built-in cabinet divides the living room from the dining room on the first floor. The master bedroom and master bath are on the second floor, directly above the dining and living rooms.

The home's furnishings are a combination of custom-designed elements, including the dining table and light fixtures in the dining room and master bedroom, and classic modern objects by Florence Knoll. The designers cleverly created a lounge from three conjoined Knoll club chairs with arms and backs removed. The palette of interior surfaces includes maple plywood cabinets and panels, plaster, aluminum leaf, and translucent glass.

One of the client's most important requests was to display two six-panel Japanese screens dating from the 17th century. On the southeast side of the house, the architects created a three-story volume sheathed in redwood. In this bay, the architects created two niches to hold the antique screens. These niches serve to divide the living space on all three levels, and are further expressed on the house's exterior with the redwood cladding. The niches divide the living room from the dining room and the master bedroom from the master bathroom, and define the width of the windows' main banks.

The owners also have an extensive collection of 18th-century Japanese wood block prints that are displayed at various wall locations. Facing Page: **The front entrance of the house features a cantilevered trellis, constructed of steel and redwood. A site wall separates the front walkway from a ten-foot change in elevation.**

The front of the house presents a simple series of volumes, rendered in wood and brick. The wood volume contains the front closet, bathroom, and rear foyer on the first floor. The two-story brick volume is the main structure of the house and appears more vertical as the elevation drops at the rear of the site. The garage appears on the right.

This Page: The fireplace surround is constructed of plaster and finished with aluminum leaf and a pewter stain. Facing Page: The architect designed the dining room table to complement the space. Custom cabinets separate the dining area from the living area.

Facing Page: **The bathroom features a wooden Japanese soaking tub. A window above the tub provides views of the woods.**

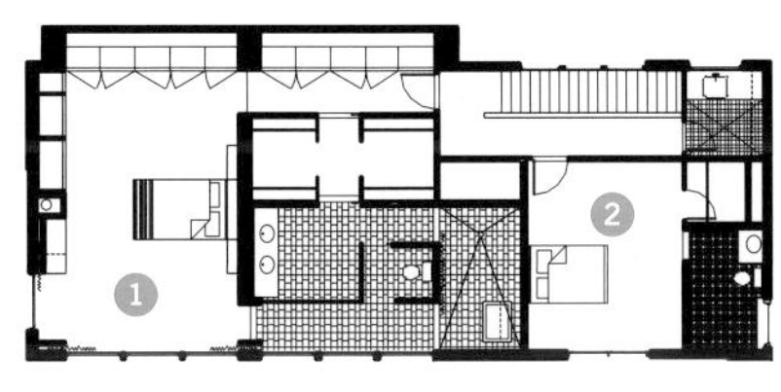

Second floor plan

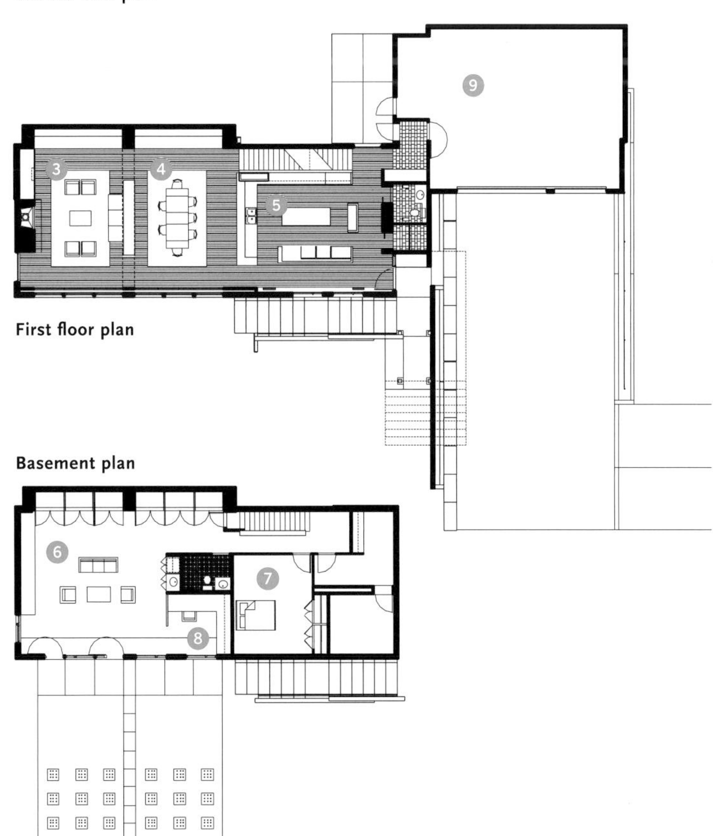

First floor plan

Basement plan

1. Master Bedroom
2. Guest Room
3. Living Room
4. Dining Room
5. Kitchen
6. Family Room
7. Guest Room
8. Study
9. Garage

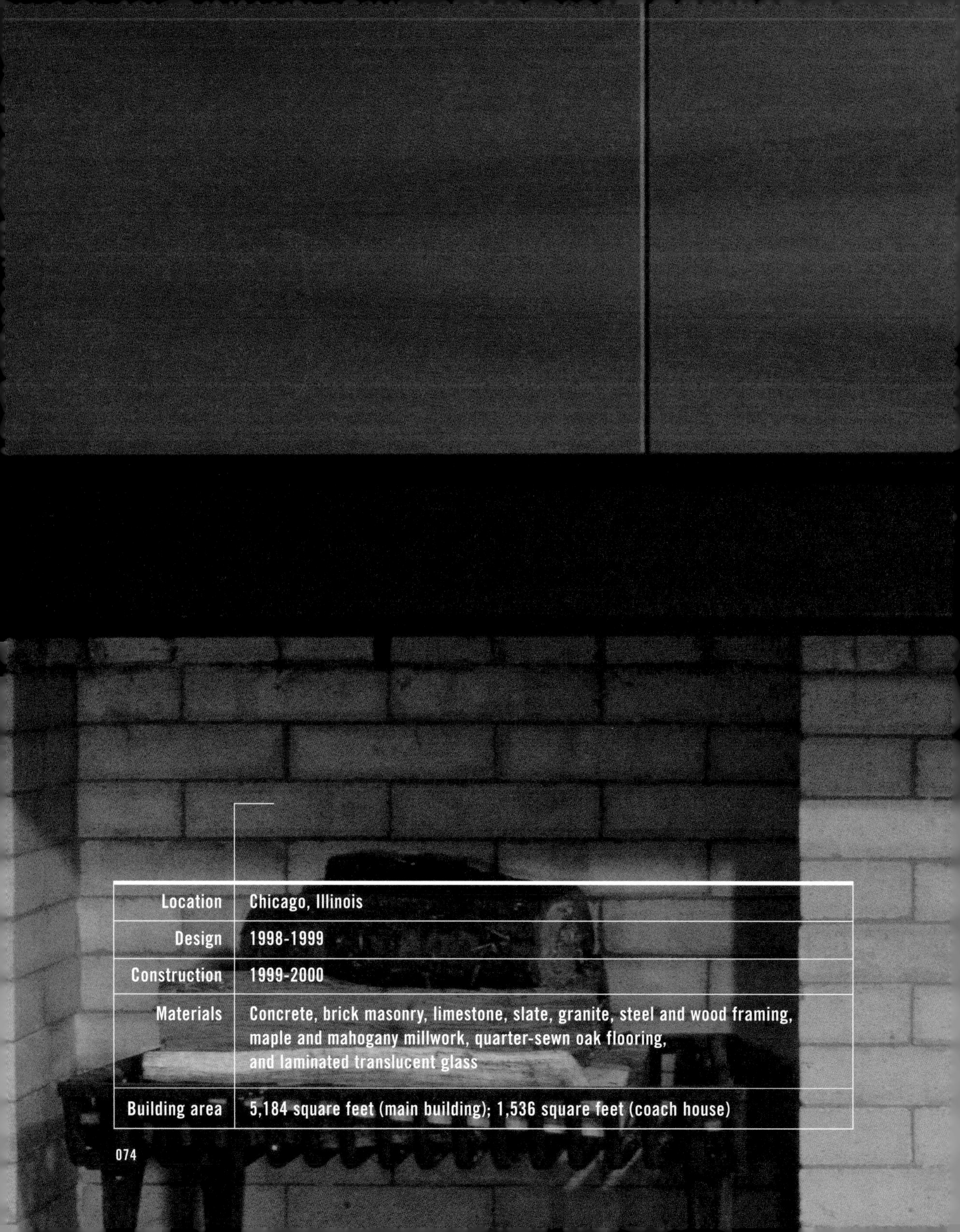

Location	Chicago, Illinois
Design	1998-1999
Construction	1999-2000
Materials	Concrete, brick masonry, limestone, slate, granite, steel and wood framing, maple and mahogany millwork, quarter-sewn oak flooring, and laminated translucent glass
Building area	5,184 square feet (main building); 1,536 square feet (coach house)

PRIVATE RESIDENCE

PRIVATE RESIDENCE

Brininstool + Lynch renovated a three-story 19th-century building in Chicago's Old Town neighborhood into street-level retail space with a residence on the top two floors. Following the Secretary of the Interior's historic preservation guidelines, the architects restored the limestone façade—which is listed on the National Register of Historic Places—while removing the entire interior structure of the house to open it up and maximize natural light. They redesigned the windows on the front façade to match the historic frames; on the rear façade, they removed two-thirds of an existing masonry wall and added a new wood-wrapped structural steel frame and a new window configuration.

The architects also renovated an existing coach house at the rear of the lot, separated from the main house by an interior courtyard, into a two-car garage and guesthouse with a full kitchen and two bedrooms with a shared bath on the second floor. In good weather, the kitchen of the coach house opens onto the courtyard with sliding glass doors, transforming the space into an outdoor entertaining and dining area. A stairway of steel, slate, wood, and glass begins at the hallway on the first floor and terminates under the skylight on the third floor. The second floor contains the dining room, kitchen, and living room. On the third floor are the master bedroom and bath, both overlooking the courtyard.

The interior palette features simple but warm materials. The floors are quarter sewn red oak in the main rooms, Vermont slate in the hallways and bathrooms, and cork in the kitchen. Living spaces are defined by custom-designed maple, mahogany, and birch wood panels that double as shelving and storage units; other custom-designed maple and mahogany cabinets in the kitchen and dining room conceal television sets and appliances. All the bedrooms feature custom, built-in maple bureaus.

The rear of the house overlooks the courtyard, a tranquil urban refuge that maintains the soothing interior palette of the main house. The architects completely excavated and repaved the courtyard in concrete, and added comfortable concrete benches interspersed with new landscaping. Small lighting fixtures placed along a flower bed to the south illuminate a walkway connecting the guesthouse to the main house. Facing Page: **Floor to ceiling windows provide views of the courtyard behind the residence.**

Sheer and opaque curtains can be recessed into the dining room millwork when they are not in use.

A translucent glass laylight above the stair allows both natural and artificial light to filter down to the second floor.

1. Living Room
2. Elevator
3. Kitchen
4. Dining Room
5. Study
6. Master Bedroom

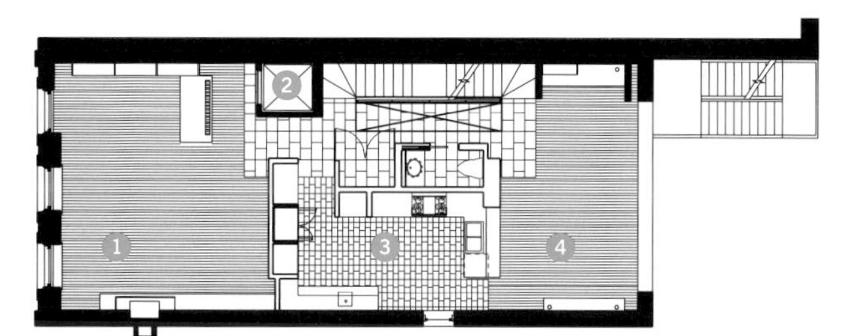

Second floor plan

Third floor plan

Front elevation

Rear elevation

Location	Chicago, Illinois
Design	1998-1999
Construction	1999-2000
Materials	Structural steel, precast concrete deck, architectural precast concrete and iron spot brick, aluminum windows, clear and translucent glass, terrazzo and gypsum board wall and ceiling systems
Building area	110,000 square feet

1440 SOUTH MICHIGAN AVENUE

1440 SOUTH MICHIGAN AVENUE

The classic courtyard buildings common throughout Chicago's residential neighborhoods before World War II inspired this 110,000-square-foot residential development. The building is arranged in a U shape around a well-defined, landscaped inner courtyard that serves as the main entry point and principal view for most units. The building's orientation also maximizes views of the Loop, the lake, and Michigan Avenue.

The project consists of two 50-unit buildings joined together along an east-west axis, at the curve of the U. Each building has a separate, defined entrance lobby off the entry courtyard, one on the north side, one on the south. This organization reduces the length of the corridors and makes the building's amenities, including covered parking for 97 cars, storage, roof terraces, and the garden, more easily accessible.

The project incorporates eight studios measuring 600 square feet; 36 one-bedroom apartments (680 to 750 square feet); 12 one-bedroom units with dens (800 square feet); 38 two-bedroom units (1,000 to 1,100 square feet); and six three-bedroom units (1,499 square feet). The apartments have a loft-like feeling created by exposed structural elements, high ceilings, and open plans. The architects provided each unit with full-height glazing along its entire perimeter. Most units have views of the city or the lakefront; others overlook the courtyard, which is naturally landscaped with birch trees, ornamental grasses, and other low-lying plants. Many units have large, open terraces, while all others have balconies.

Instead of the poured-in-place concrete frame with deep foundations typically used for residential projects of this scale, the architect designed a steel and precast concrete structure, based on the building's size and the soil's bearing capacity. Since the budget limited the cladding options, a cheaper window wall system was selected instead of curtain wall, to open up the units to the outdoors. The brick skin is a reference to Chicago's domestic vernacular. Previous Pages: **Glass-enclosed retail space and screened parking are located in the base of the building. Typical residential units feature a window wall. Set back penthouses feature large roof terraces. A central garden is accessed by four brick stair towers.** Facing Page: **Typical units feature balconies, full-height glazing, and grilles for through-wall HVAC units. Set back penthouses feature sun-screens and large roof terraces.**

Location	Chicago Illinois
Design	1993
Construction	1993-2001
Materials	Poured concrete columns; reinforced, two-way, flat concrete slabs; clear anodized aluminum windows; clear and translucent glass; honed black granite and pre-finished metal siding
Building area	152,000 square feet

700 WEST VAN BUREN

700 WEST VAN BUREN

This prominent, 16-story residential tower overlooks Chicago's busiest expressway interchange and marks the southwest corner of the city's central business district. Given its particular siting, the architects considered how the building would appear to motorists and pedestrians alike. The building appears particularly dominating to drivers on the north-south expressway, since the expressway, while not underground, is sunken 20 feet below street level.

The architects broke the multi-story base, which contains parking, commercial space, and the residential lobby, into two parts. The lower portion is clad in a combination of transparent and opaque glass that defines the residential lobby, retail facilities, and building services; the upper part is a partially open architectural louver system that screens the 105-space parking garage from view while still allowing light to enter the space. Canopied storefronts running north along Des Plaines Avenue, direct visitors to a glass vestibule that is flanked on the north by a back-lit loading dock structure. The loading dock is wrapped in translucent glass panels that match the glass over the door and on the storefront. The metal siding used on the exterior continues into the lobby's interior, where the architects positioned it opposite an exposed concrete wall.

Inside the lobby, eight-foot sycamore panels, lit from behind, appear to float in front of the concrete wall and extend to the walls and ceiling of the elevator lobby. The tiny, 196-square-foot main lobby, which projects from the southern metal panel-clad wall, features a perforated metal ceiling. A cocoa-colored mat is set into the black terrazzo of the lobby floors. Most of the lobby's materials continue in the building's exterior skin, except the terrazzo and sycamore, which balance the warmer, more textured materials.

The 110,000-square-foot tower is enclosed in a full-height window system, with various configurations that break down the massing and define an asymmetrical penthouse element. Inside are 97 units, ten per floor, ranging in size from 670-square-foot one-bedroom units to 1,600-square-foot duplex penthouses. With inset balconies and full-height sliding glass doors, each residential unit opens to panoramic views of the city and Lake Michigan. The majority of the balconies are located at the corners to ensure privacy. The duplex penthouses on the 15th floor incorporate expansive roof terraces. Instead of using exterior railings to enclose the terraces, the designers used 3 1/2-by-2-foot fiberglass planters. On the eastern façade, the concrete piers supporting the roof and sun-screen separate each terrace; on the western façade, wide poured-concrete planters separate the large terraces. Previous Pages: **Typical residential floors feature exposed concrete columns, full-height window walls, aluminum slab covers, and grilles at through wall HVAC units. Top floors are set-back duplex penthouse units with roof terraces.** Facing Page: **The design provides a canopy over the street-level retail space, which leads to the residential entry and adjacent loading dock and garage entry. Louvered semi-screened parking levels are located between the retail level and the residential floors.**

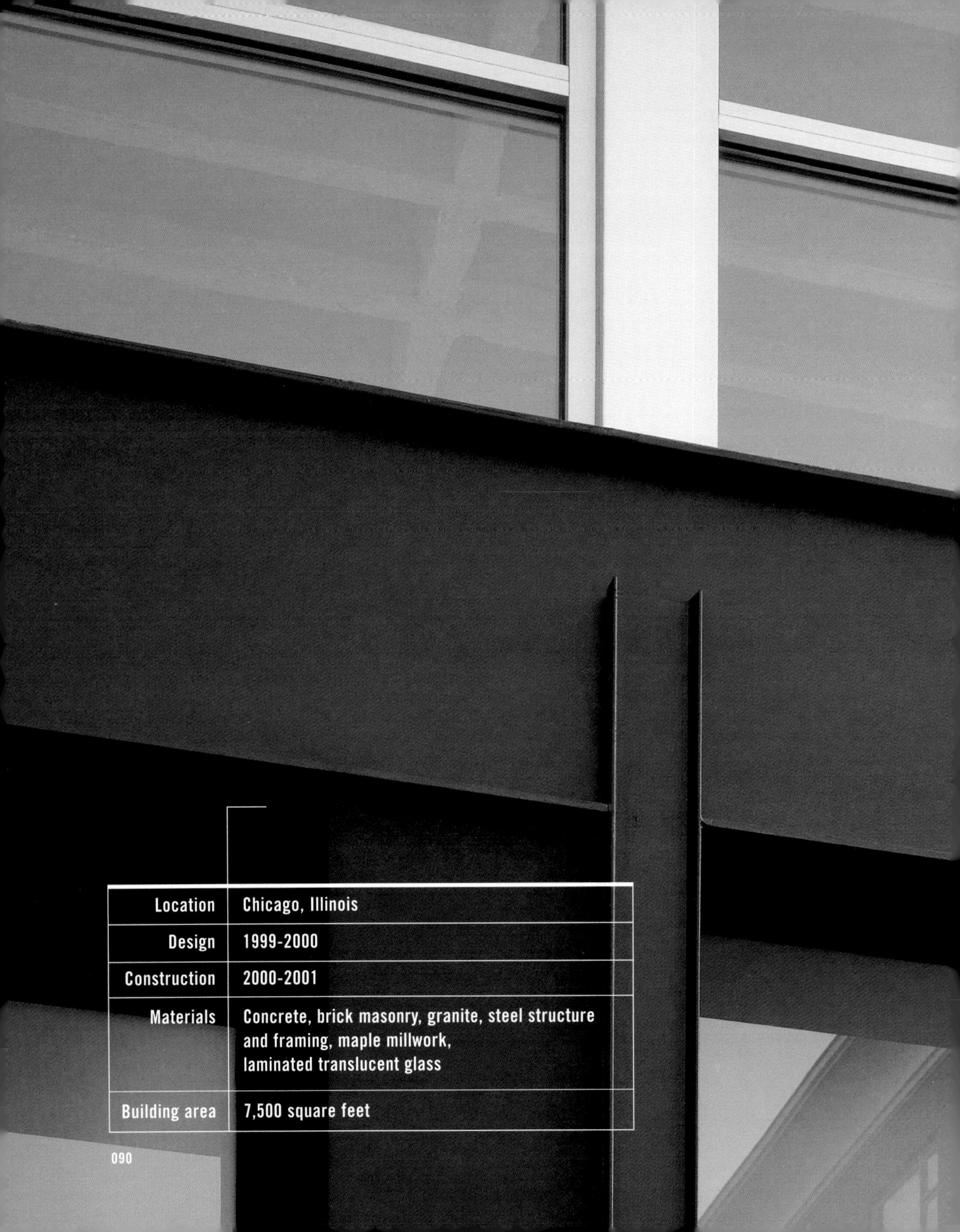

Location	Chicago, Illinois
Design	1999-2000
Construction	2000-2001
Materials	Concrete, brick masonry, granite, steel structure and framing, maple millwork, laminated translucent glass
Building area	7,500 square feet

SQUARK

SQUARK

A small group of theoretical physicists created Squark, a company that provides partial differential equations calculated by a "super computer" over the internet. To house their small offices, the company chose a modest, three-story, 7,500-square-foot brick building on Chicago's West Side.

Squark currently occupies the building's third floor and basement, but will shortly expand into the first and second floors. Brininstool + Lynch's design joins lab and office space in a comfortable work environment that has plenty of natural light and views of downtown Chicago, and presents a streamlined, organized face to clients and visitors. The design also integrates the client's needs for complex HVAC, electronics, and communication systems.

The existing building's façade had been altered extensively since it was built in the 1920s. The storefront had been filled in with wood framing and siding, with awning windows at the top. Much of the building's terra-cotta ornamentation had been removed, the limestone cladding on the upper two stories was falling away, and the parapet was falling over. The architects decided to remove what was left of the building's original façade, and to have the yellow brick masonry on the remaining three sides tuck-pointed—the bricks realigned with new mortar. They added a new skin of brick, steel, aluminum, and glass on the façade and replaced the face brick on the west elevation with a common yellow brick that is similar in color to the new façade brick.

The designers established a new entrance from the side parking lot, which becomes the de facto main entrance to the entire building. The position of a new elevator at the building's rear places the lobby of each floor near the computer lab, and lets visitors see the company's working areas before arriving at the offices. This gesture reflects the company's philosophy that work is of paramount importance to its image.

The basement houses the computer room and special equipment; the third floor houses a reception area, computer laboratory, two adjacent semi-private work areas, a pair of bathrooms, a kitchen, an open office area, and a conference room, which spans the entire width of the building. The conference room is wrapped in floor-to-ceiling glass on the south side and boasts windows with views to the Loop on the east side. A maple volume surrounded by translucent and transparent glass separates the open offices from the conference room. The company plans to use the remaining two floors for future growth.

Since the floor plate is small, the architects created the illusion of greater space by dividing all interior functions with warm wood-clad volumes or glass walls. Polished concrete or carpeted floors and an off-white paint palette create the illusion of a large, continuous space.

The architects used translucent glass at the front entry (at right) and the storefront. Original concrete floors and brick masonry can be seen through the second floor windows.

This Page: **The conference room features a wood wall surrounded by translucent and clear glass. A tiered soffit defines circulation throughout the floor and houses HVAC, computer and communications cables, and ambient lighting.** Facing Page: **The designers juxtaposed old and new materials in the wall that separates the office area from the conference room.**

The translucent glass wall (at right) separates the computer area from the office corridor.

1. Conference
2. Office
3. Workstation
4. Computer Room

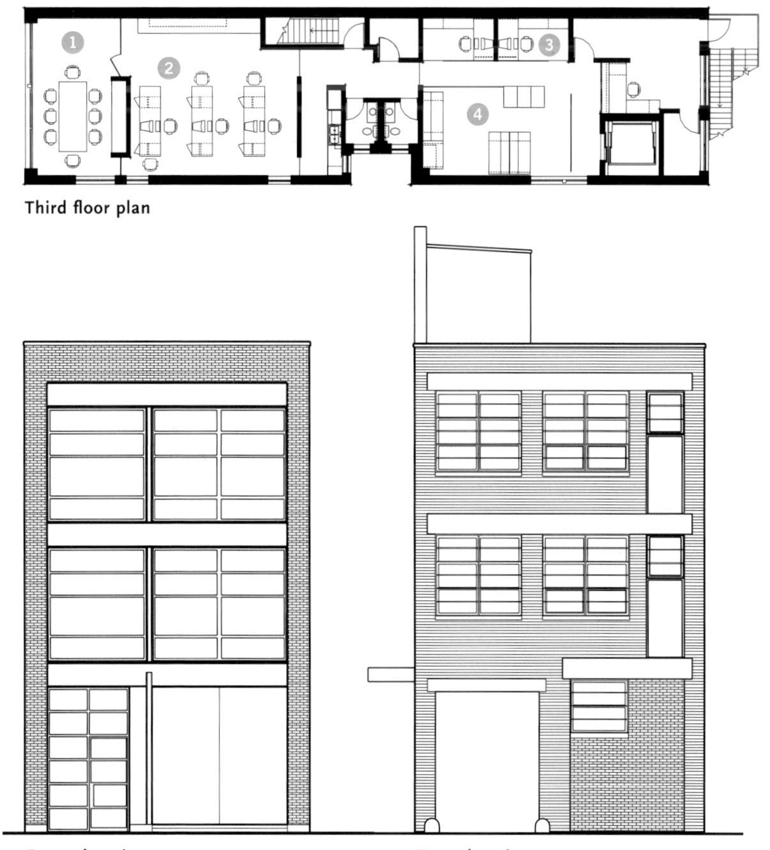

Third floor plan

Front elevation

Rear elevation

Location	Chicago, Illinois
Design	2000
Construction	2000-2001
Materials	French limestone, granite, maple flooring, structural steel, stainless steel panels, translucent glass
Area	2,810 square feet

WEISS RESIDENCE

WEISS RESIDENCE

The owner of this condominium in downtown Chicago asked Brininstool + Lynch to create an open and serene living environment oriented to expansive views of Lake Michigan and nearby landmarks, including the John Hancock tower and Navy Pier. The architects' biggest challenge was removing the existing structural and mechanical walls that established traditional room layouts, to transform a less roomy three-bedroom apartment into an airy two-bedroom unit.

The architects removed original partition walls between the kitchen, dining room, living room and library and established an entirely new, open, internal volume defined by partition walls separate from the building's exterior envelope. New pathways for mechanical and sprinkler systems that had previously been enclosed in partition walls now run beneath dropped ceilings.

The designers defined the new interior spaces with a carefully chosen material palette of plaster ceilings and walls of plaster-covered drywall and translucent glass. Stained maple wood floors visually distinguish the living areas from the floors of the circulation and utility areas, which are French limestone. The translucent glass walls defining the master bathroom create a luminous interior volume visible from the entrance hallway or master bedroom, and bring natural light into an otherwise dark interior. The custom steel and French limestone bathtub and sinks are both esthetic focal points and utilitarian objects. The dining table, which is cantilevered from the wall, is designed to give the appearance of a stone slab floating above the sill. Similarly, a custom light fixture above the dining table appears to float below the ceiling beam.

All of the apartment's custom millwork and storage units were designed and detailed as parts of the walls–rather than cabinetry–to reinforce the idea that an entirely new architectural volume has been inserted within the shell of the existing apartment. Previous pages: **The media room features translucent glass sliding panels.** Facing Page: **The architect designed the stainless steel and limestone dining table, as well as the aluminum light fixture.**

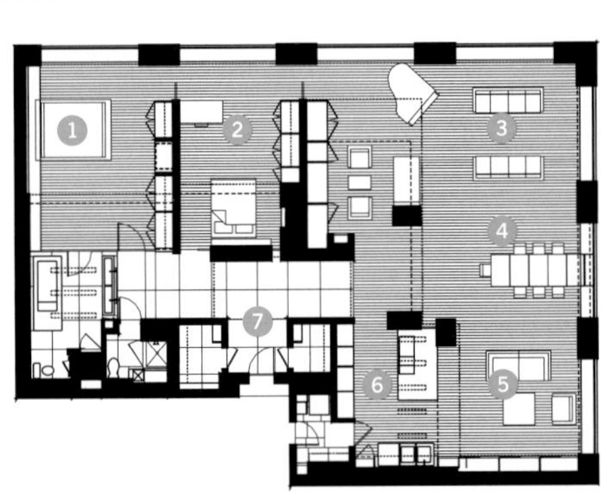

The kitchen sink is constructed of steel and limestone.

Facing page: **The master bedroom features stained maple wood floors and abundant natural light.**
This page: **The custom steel and French limestone sinks and bathtub are both esthetic focal points and utilitarian objects.**

Location	Chicago Illinois
Design	2000-2001
Construction	2001-2002
Materials	Tinted clear and translucent glass; aluminum window wall; aluminum curtain wall; concrete, pre-finished metal panels and grating
Building area	200,000 square feet

1845 SOUTH MICHIGAN AVENUE

1845 SOUTH MICHIGAN AVENUE

In designing this commercial and residential tower in downtown Chicago, the architects responded to opposing programmatic requirements: the minimum foundation system supporting the maximum building. In order to meet Chicago's zoning ordinance, the design had to accommodate apartments and a parking lot within a structure limited to 185 feet in height. Although the surrounding buildings range from two to seven stories on average, the overall nature of the Michigan Avenue area encourages taller projects. A pair of residential structures just one block south of the site top out at 28 and 30 stories; several blocks north, the street is filled with mostly high-rise towers that are expanding south. In response to these factors, the architects developed a 20-story, post-tensioned concrete structure that allows for column-free residential space and requires only 24 caissons to support floor plates as large as 12,800 square feet.

A five-story base that maintains the street wall along Michigan Avenue holds a parking structure for 105 cars, a lobby for the condominium tower, and a retail arcade; a surface lot behind the building, accessed by an alley, accommodates an additional 30 cars. The base is clad in bands of materials that vary in translucency and opacity. Clear anodized aluminum panels enclose the garage from the sixth-floor terrace to the top of a contrasting aluminum canopy over the entrance. Below the canopy, the façade is wrapped in back-lit translucent glass, and, below that, a wire-cloth scrim that provides a safety barrier between the sidewalk and the slightly sunken retail arcade, while maintaining visibility.

The architects exposed the lobby, a honed black granite-clad volume floating on a light gray slate floor, through expanses of transparent glass along the street. By using the same materials that define the exterior of the building for the lobby's interior, they created continuity between inside and out. The south wall, for example, is an extension of the exposed concrete wall separating the lobby and retail arcade. The north wall is also made of exposed concrete, but accented with Anigre wood panels that wrap behind the granite volume.

The 140 residential units in the tower offer commanding views of downtown Chicago and Lake Michigan through floor-to-ceiling glass on the east and west elevations. The one- and two-bedroom units range in size from 650 to 1,200 square feet, and feature nine-foot-high ceilings, except those on the top floor, which have 12-foot ceiling heights. Many of the interior walls are made of exposed concrete, like the tower's north and south faces, giving the units a slightly loft-like character.

Previous Pages: **A depressed retail arcade (at right) is set back six feet from the metal screen at street level. The residential lobby features clear full-height glass. At the north end of the building, a back-lit translucent volume accommodates utility meters and services. The garage enclosure is four stories high and composed of horizontal metal panels with vertical breaks and metal screening.**

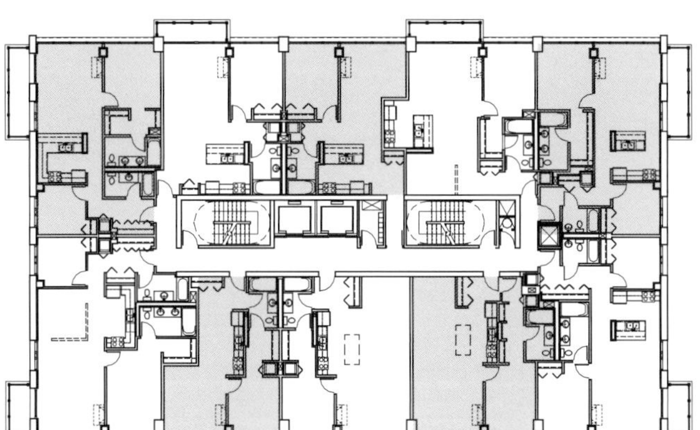

Typical residential floor plan

(Top) This computer-generated image provides a view looking north to Grant Park and the Loop.
(Bottom, right) The tower is set back at the sixth floor and the columns are left exposed.
Typical residential floors feature a floor to ceiling window wall and columns with matching slab-covers.
The elevation is topped out by a full-length sunscreen.

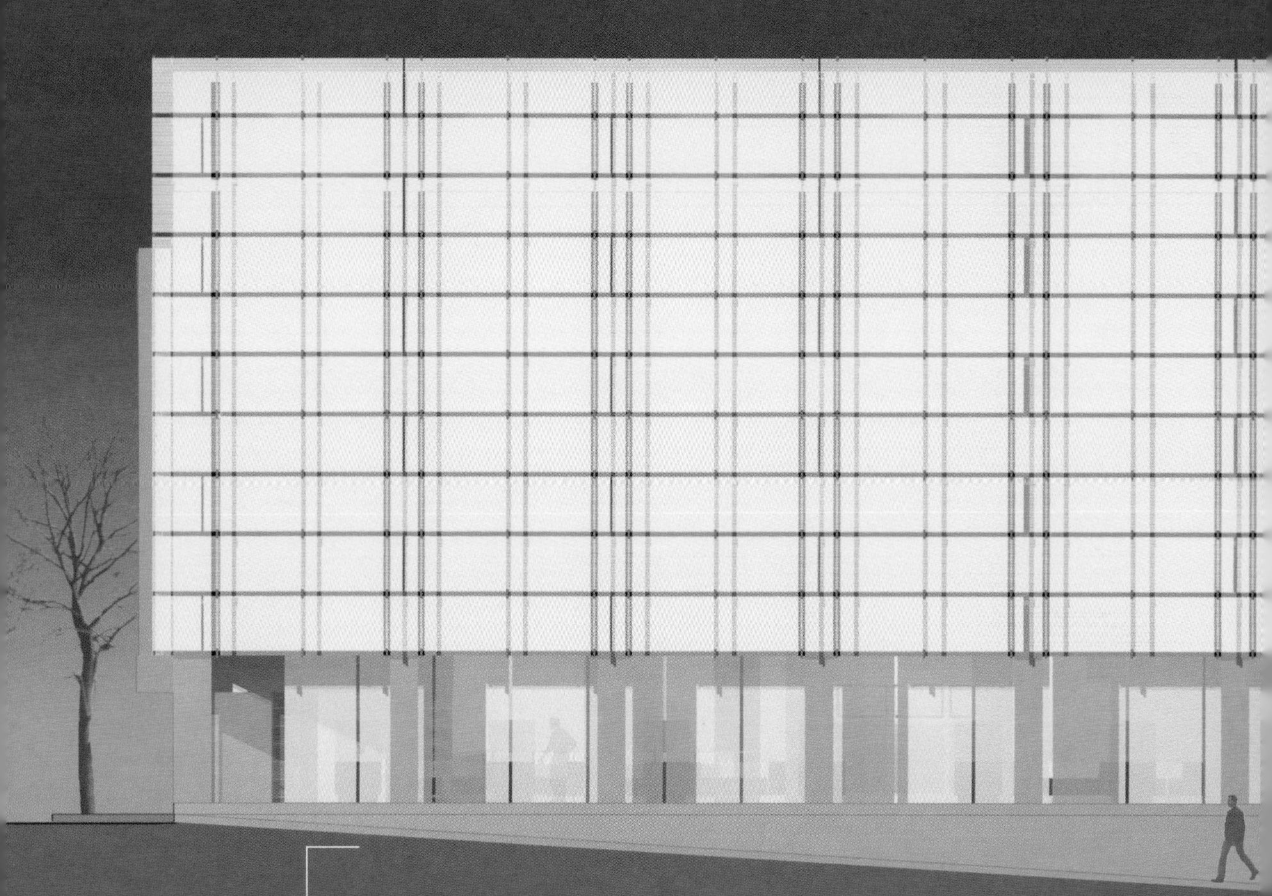

Location	Racine, Wisconsin
Design	1999-2000
Construction	2000-2003
Materials	Poured-in-place concrete, limestone, structural steel framing systems, custom aluminum curtain wall, laminated translucent glass, acrylic cladding, reconstituted white ash, rubber flooring, veneer plaster
Building area	46,326 square feet

RACINE ART MUSEUM

RACINE ART MUSEUM

Over the past 30 years, the downtown core of Racine, an industrial city in southeastern Wisconsin on the western shore of Lake Michigan, has experienced a physical and economic decline. The art museum is one of many projects planned to revitalize downtown Racine.

The architects gutted and transformed an existing 19th-century limestone structure that has served may functions over the years, and still contains the structural elements of seven buildings, some dating back to the Civil War. With contemporary materials, the architects developed an elegant, well-crafted environment for the display of contemporary art, focusing on ceramics, fiber, glass, metal, and wood. The new 40,000-square-foot facility will include 8,500 square feet of exhibition galleries, a museum store, library and research areas, art storage and preparation spaces, offices, and various support operations.

The project's modest budget prohibited the architects from repairing or completely replacing the building's existing limestone cladding. Instead, they decided to wrap the limestone façades in a durable, inexpensive, and attractive new skin, composed of double-wall acrylic panels set within a custom steel frame and raised 18 inches off the existing limestone surface with steel clips.

The acrylic panels will have an iridescent quality during the day; at night, artificial lighting mounted on the top of the façade will illuminate the new acrylic façade, making the building glow. A large steel frame placed above the entry doors will emphasize the main entrance. Multimedia video screens mounted on the frame will display images of the museum's offerings and information about its exhibitions. Along the ground floor, the architects replaced existing store-front windows with a continuous curtain wall that will provide views of interior displays and the museum store from the street.

1 Office
2 Storage
3 Lobby
4 Gallery One
5 Gallery Two
6 Gallery Three

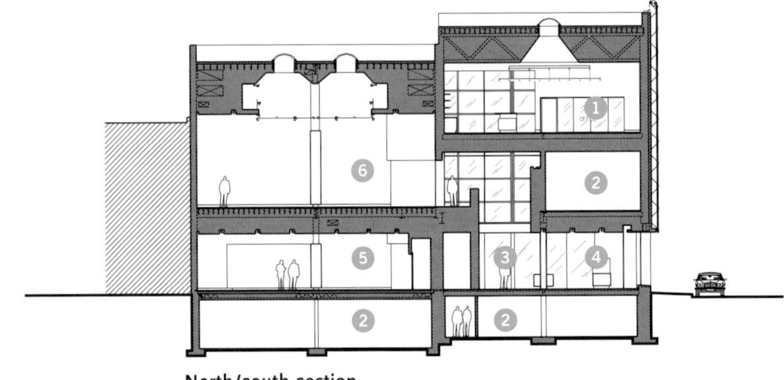

North/south section

Visitors will enter through a two-story atrium with a grand stairway leading to the second floor, where large, double-height exhibition galleries and an art library and research facility will be located. The architects created a new courtyard at the rear of the first floor by removing old additions to the original building. The third floor will be devoted to museum offices, meeting rooms, and support services; the basement will house art preparation and storage. The first floor gallery will have interior butt-glazed translucent laminated glass running east-west on the south side of the gallery. Within the galleries, flexible lighting will provide the consistent light quality that is essential to art display.

The architects defined the interior volumes by linking existing structural elements with new wall, floor, and ceiling planes. The backbone of the interior architecture is a set of millwork volumes that incorporate art and video displays, shelving, workstations in the library and offices, and all lighting and wiring. Other interior finishes include white ash, laminated translucent glass, clear acrylic, perforated metal, plastic laminate, aluminum channel, and plastic resin. This Page and Facing Page: **These sections show how the architects combined buildings and structures, removed floors, and added ceilings to accommodate new functional requirements, as well as new interior proportions.**

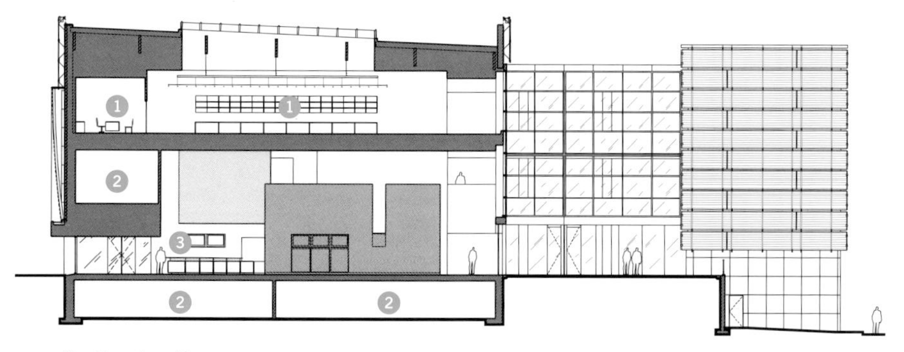

East/west section

Facing Page: **An old structure was demolished adjacent to the courtyard and glass curtainwall.**
This Page: **Illuminated donor panels and video information screens are recessed into the stairwell. The display cases (at right) are anchored to the columns, so that they appear to float above the floor.**

The front entry is underneath a canopy, which features video modules behind the canted steel and fabric panels. Glazing on the first floor allows passers-by to see into the museum and the bookstore (at left).

CREDITS

700 WEST VAN BUREN CHICAGO, ILLINOIS

Design Principal
David Brininstool

Project Architect
Matthew Reiskin

Project Team
Mary English, Jason Longo

Civil Engineer
Terra Engineering, Ltd.

General Contractor
E.W. Corrigan Construction Company

MEP Engineer
WMA Consulting Engineers, Ltd.

Structural Engineer
C. E. Anderson & Associates

Client
Keating Group

1440 S. MICHIGAN AVENUE CHICAGO, ILLINOIS

Design Principal
David Brininstool

Project Architect
Matthew Reiskin

Project Team
Pablo Diaz, Mary English

General Contractor
CMK Metropoitan Construction Corp.

Structural Engineer
Stearn-Joglekar, Ltd.

Client
CMK Development

1845 S. MICHIGAN AVENUE CHICAGO, ILLINOIS

Design Principal
David Brininstool

Project Architect
Matthew Reiskin

Project Team
Joanna Dabek, Jason Longo

Civil Engineer
Terra Engineering, Ltd.

General Contractor
Norcon, Inc.

MEP Engineer
McGuire Engineers

Structural Engineer
C.E. Anderson & Associates

Client
CMK Development

BURKHARDT RESIDENCE BRIDGMAN, MICHIGAN

Design Principal
David Brininstool

General Contractor
Gray Carlson

Client
Susan Burkhardt

Photographer
Jamie Padgett, Karant + Associates

CHICAGO RECORDING CO. CHICAGO, ILLINOIS

Design Principal
Brad Lynch

Project Architect
Jason Longo

General Contractor
Turner Special Projects

Sound
Cleon Wells

Structural Engineer
Stearn-Joglekar

Client
Chicago Recording Company

Photographer
Jamie Padgett, Karant + Associates

CORUS BANK HEADQUARTERS CHICAGO, ILLINOIS

Design Principal
Brad Lynch

Project Architect
Daniel Martus

Project Team
David Brininstool, Jason Longo, Keith Ginnodo

General Contractor
Beacon/Skanska Construction

MEP Engineer
Klaucens & Associates

Structural Engineer
Stearn-Joglekar

Structural Engineer/Stone
Klein and Hoffman

Client
Corus Bankshares

Photographer
Jamie Padgett, Padgett and Company

LISKA & ASSOCIATES CHICAGO, ILLINOIS

Design Principal
Brad Lynch

Project Architect
Jason Longo

General Contractor
Progress Construction

Millwork
Dovetail Woodworking Studio

Client
Steve Liska

Photographer
Jamie Padgett, Padgett and Company

PERIMETER GALLERY CHICAGO, ILLINOIS

Design Principal
Brad Lynch

General Contractor
Goldberg General Contracting

Client
Perimeter Gallery

Photographer
Jamie Padgett, Karant + Associates

PERIMETER GALLERY NEW YORK, NEW YORK

Design Principal
Brad Lynch

Project Architect
Christine Marsal Brandl

General Contractor
Ed Bennett

Client
Perimeter Gallery

Photographer
Chris Barrett, Hendrich Blessing

PRIVATE RESIDENCE
CHICAGO, ILLINOIS

Design Principal
Brad Lynch

Project Architect
Kristen Rozycki

Project Team
Tom Dilley,
Christine Marsal Brandl

General Contractor
Bell Construction

Structural Engineer
Lyle Haag Engineering

Client
Name Withheld at
Owner's Request

Photographer
Jamie Padgett,
Padgett and Company

RACINE ART MUSEUM
RACINE, WISCONSIN

Design Principal
Brad Lynch

Managing Principal
David Brininstool

Project Architect
Pablo Diaz

Project Manager
Daniel Martus

Project Team
Christine Marsal Brandl,
Jason Longo,
Mary English

General Contractor
Bukacek Construction Inc.

Structural and MEP
Engineers
Arnold and O'Sheridan, Inc.

Client
Wustum Museum Art
Association

SQUARK
CHICAGO, ILLINOIS

Design Principal
Brad Lynch

Project Architect
Kevin Southard

General Contractor
Goldberg General
Contracting, Inc.

Structural Engineer
Lyle Haag Engineering
and Moshe Calamaro
& Associates

Client
Estia Eichten and
Deborah Forman

Photographer
Chris Barrett,
Hedrich Blessing

THOMPSON RESIDENCE
CHICAGO, ILLINOIS

Design Principal
Brad Lynch

Project Team
David Brininstool,
Anthony Manzo

Construction Manager
Brininstool + Lynch

Client
J.A. and Ellie Thompson

Photographer
Jamie Padgett,
Karant + Associates

UNION TOWER
CHICAGO, ILLINOIS

Design Principals
Brad Lynch,
David Brininstool

Project Architect
Matthew Reiskin

Project Team
Jason Longo

Associate Architect
OWP&P

MEP Engineer
Environmental Sytems
Design, Inc.

Structural Engineer
OWP&P

Client
Development Resources,
Inc.

Photographer
Darris Harris,
Padgett and Company

WEISS RESIDENCE
CHICAGO, ILLINOIS

Design Principal
Brad Lynch

Project Architect
Kristen Rozycki

Project Manager
Tom Basset Dilley

Project Team
Christine Marsal Brandl,
Kevin Southard

General Contractor
Bell Construction

Millwork
Village Woodsmiths

Steelwork
VK Ferro Design

Client
Adrienne Weiss

Photographer
Chris Barrett,
Hendrich Blessing

YAMAMOTO RESIDENCE
MCCORDSVILLE, INDIANA

Design Principal
Brad Lynch

Project Architect
Andrea Zaff

Project Team
Keith Ginnodo,
Jason Longo,
Christine Marsal Brandl

General Contractor
Lerchen, Inc.

Structural Engineer
Stearn-Joglekar

Client
Tom and Nancy Yamamoto

Photographer
Chris Barrett,
Hedrich Blessing

THANKS

Both David Brininstool and I are from the Midwest and intentionally chose Chicago as our destination to work, inspired by a profound respect for the city's architecture. For us, Chicago has been the culmination of an original American mind-set, and nowhere is that more apparent than in its buildings of the last 125 years. Since the great fire, frenzies of building have led to the development of ideas in Chicago's architecture, some important, others unfortunate, but almost always through building. This is appropriate, after all, since architecture is a "building" art. Similarly, our work has developed and improved on a project by project basis, as a result of the building process.

We drafted our first project by hand in an apartment near Wrigley Field; today, our current offices in River North use advanced computer software. Over the years, the work and circumstances have changed, while our lives and the lives of those around us have tenaciously evolved. This evolution and development will continue, although it would be an arduous task without the involvement of our associates, Dan Martus, Matthew Reiskin, Pablo Diaz, Tom Bassett Dilley, and Kevin Southard, in addition to the many others who have contributed to our success while working in our office. Similarly, there would be no Brininstool + Lynch without the sustenance and trust placed in us by our families, friends, clients, and consultants, and in particular by Karen Carter.

Raul Barreneche, who has had a generous interest in our work over the years, initiated the idea of this monograph. We thank him for his support and his clarity of words. From our office, we would like to thank Christine Marsal Brandl for patiently compiling materials, while continuing to contribute her talent in architecture to our office. —**Brad Lynch**